Sarcasm

Cheryl **Caldwell**

KPT PUBLISHING

Some people
get on your last
nerve.

Do you ever have the urge to tell someone to shut up ...when they aren't even talking?

OK...most people
get on your last nerve.

7 Billion people on the planet and I can deal with about 3 of them.

You try to be patient
and then....

Don't like my sarcasm?
Well, I don't like your stupid.

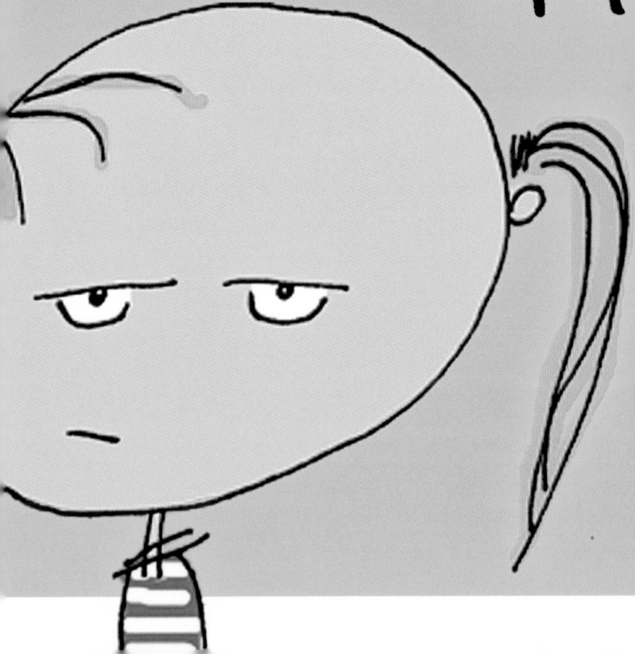

You excuse them.

C

Everything happens
for a reason.

Sometimes
that reason is
you're stupid,
and you make
bad choices.

They think
you're being mean,
when in truth...

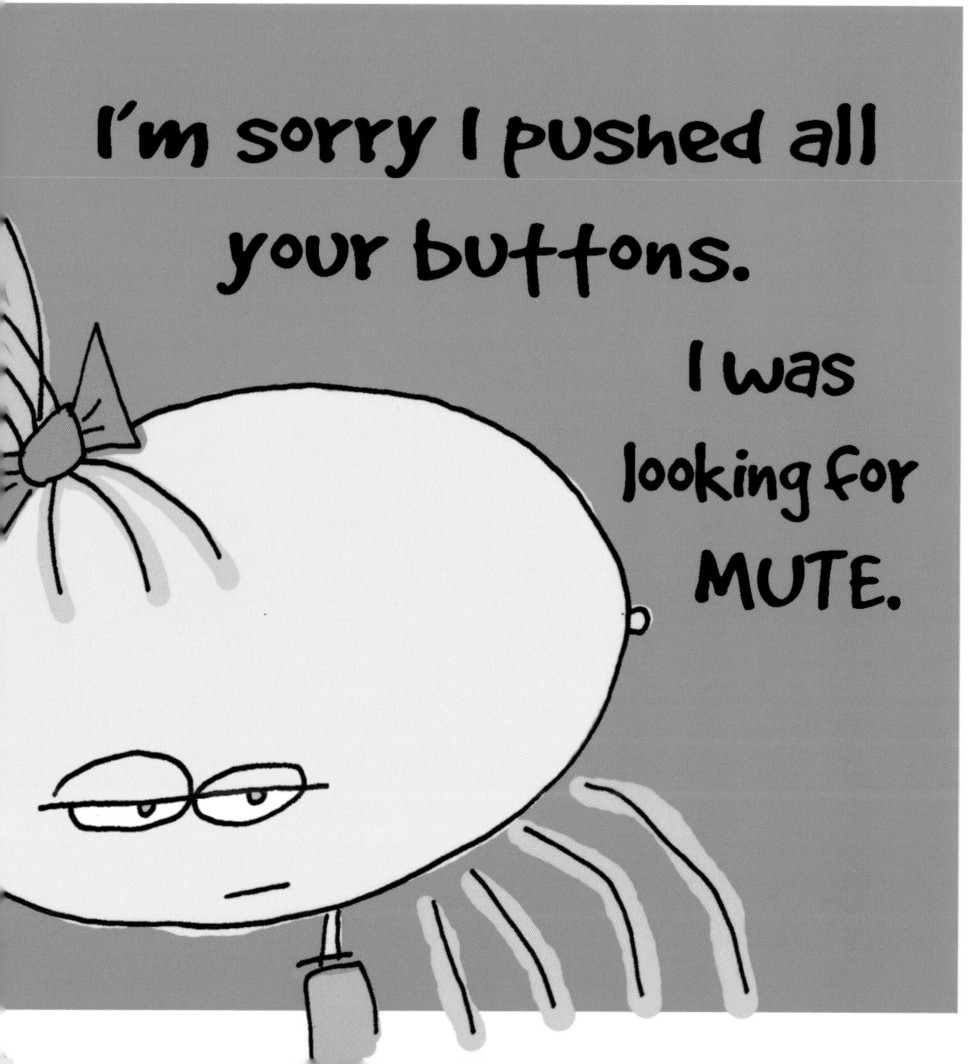
I'm sorry I pushed all your buttons.
I was looking for MUTE.

Sometimes it's
just too early to deal.

You try to be encouraging.

Some people need
a
HIGH FIVE.

In the face.
With a chair.

Because you're
helpful like that.

Some people are like old TVs...
You have to hit them
up side the head
a few times
before they
get the picture.

You are often
misunderstood.

But you know
you are not alone.

It's quite possibly
a medical condition.

They misread your behavior

"If you can't say anything nice, don't say anything at all."

And people wonder why I'm so quiet.

and misinterpret
your intentions.

I'm a pacifist alright...
I'm about to pass a fist across your face.

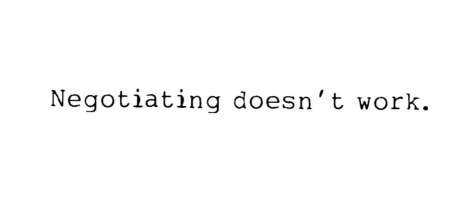

Negotiating doesn't work.

So, what can you do?

You can't
fix
STUPID

but you can
numb it
with a
2 x 4

Because regardless
of who is at fault,

you have to remember

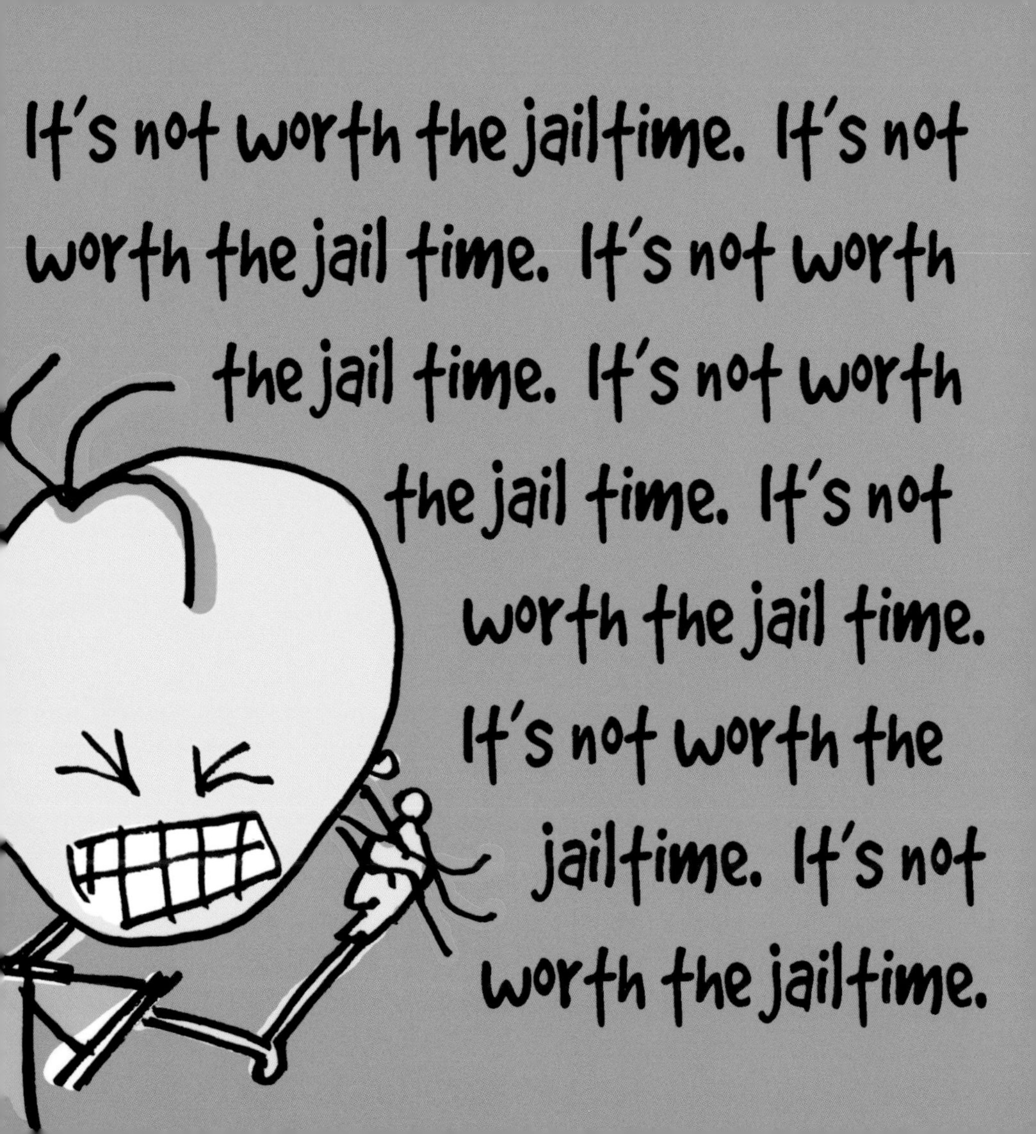
It's not worth the jailtime. It's not worth the jail time. It's not worth the jail time. It's not worth the jail time. It's not worth the jail time. It's not worth the jailtime. It's not worth the jailtime.

Instead, think of
fun ways to interact,

maintain your
sense of humor,

and apologize
when necessary.

I'm sorry
we fought.

I hate it
when
you're wrong.

You could
be called heroic.

Does it count as saving a person's life if you simply refrain from killing them?

So
take a deep breath...

PATIENCE is...

what you have when there are too many witnesses.

and say to yourself,

About the Author

Cheryl **Caldwell** is a sometimes artist, photographer, filmmaker, marine aquarist, and author. Most of her inspiration comes from her unconventional view of the world and the fact that she finds the mundane hilarious. She is owner of Co-edikit®, a humor based company that pairs comical illustrations with a witty combination of clear cut, down-to-earth words of wisdom and sarcastic humor. Her artwork and characters have been licensed and sold throughout the world. Her original paintings of the Co-edikit® characters can be found in several art galleries in the U.S., including Bee Galleries in New Orleans. She still subscribes to the philosophy that if you're having a bad day, ask a four- or five-year-old to skip. It's hysterical.

Sarcasm

Copyright © 2017 Cheryl Caldwell

Published by KPT Publishing
Minneapolis, Minnesota 55406
www.KPTPublishing.com

ISBN: 978-1-944833-22-0

Design and production by Koechel Peterson and Associates, Minneapolis, Minnesota

First printing March 2017

10 9 8 7 6 5 4 3 2 1

Printed in the United States of America